THE SPACE BETWEEN OUR FINGERTIPS

LOVE WON'T HEAL YOU, BUT IT WILL EMBRACE YOU AS YOU HEAL YOURSELF.

IRINA DUTTA

Made with ♥ on the Notion Press Platform
www.notionpress.com

Contents

Contents

PART 1

FIRST, LOVE

Walking into a new universe

falling, flying and dreaming

1. COULD I LOVE YOU ANYMORE?

It was this random day,
when emotions took the better of me
When all that mattered was talking to you
When all I longed for was the soft touch of your hand against mine,
So that we could both freak out all over again and looked like fools
In public.
When your voice was the only anchor to get me through the day
Falling in love with you was falling in so deep that it meant flying
Looking out of the window of a plane one day and realizing we were so much higher together
It was like looking at the night sky and getting intoxicated by the lights again
You were the universe in which I could stargaze forever
You said I was your sunshine, but I believed you to be my sunrays
You said I was your drizzle on cold days, to me, you were my rain in grief.
You told me I was there for you to lean on, when it was your shoulder I borrowed
You took my dreams and stuck them up in places of your tender heart no one has ever been to
Taking my broken pieces and drawing gold through their ripped edges
Slowly trying to put them back together, like kinsugi – a mystery waiting to be solved by someone intellectual

You would sit up late, if it meant catching all those stars that fell from my skies
And wishing them to get back up even in dark nights.
And I can't write enough about how special all of it made me feel.
Because perfect is what is being you.
You did what I could never do, you loved me,
And you loved me whole.
You loved me into whole.
Like I was not this broken imperfect person, the world had shaped me into
Not the wings of a dead butterfly that no longer wished to fly
Like I wasn't at all difficult to love, like it was a privilege to be me-
But it must be a privilege to be loved by you
So deeply that it wasn't even falling.
You were a supernova
All the while disguised as a white dwarf and this is still all clichés.
We breathed in clichés, dancing in cringe-
Oh how could you loved me deep? Love me whole?
We can't help it, can we?
Our clichéd love, our explosive love
And I may not be able to show you the wonder-
The wonder of being loved by someone like you
How your happening was the only coincidence i waited for all the 17 years of my life
Sometimes I think the universe plays hide and seek
Does it fight too?
To bring together things too strange and too strong to
be together And so I will love you,
Deeply, honestly, completely, genuinely.

More than anyone else could love you, I will fill
Those wounds of your dying star-heart I will stitch up every scar, with love that bleeds like
pain-
I do not need to draw gold- because gold and god is what you already are.
Just like you did, I will turn the burning house into a home
Play friends with the lost child within you
Mother your grief and write away the suicide notes to the stream
When time stops and there is only oblivion We will know we had each other to hold on to.
My death will sing your lullabies, and yours,mine
And yet all I can ever ask is could I love you anymore?

2. IN THIS DREAM

In this dream,
You hold my hand and point me towards the sunset
You teach me how to be beautiful again
We slow dance on a patch of sunlight
You call me by the name love,and i learn to say yes to heaven
In this dream, the warmth of the sun falls on my bare skin and i feel yellow for the first time
For the first time, i let love find safe space in my heart
everything is quiet and i'm at peace
You have kissed all my voices to sleep by now
And now together, we sing lullabies to our nightmares
I forget to make this poem about the black hole in my chest
In this dream, we chase behind each other like children
We giggle and paint the sun pink with our love
We get wet under the summer rain when daffodils drip with rain water
And lay barefoot on the tender muddy earth under a sky full of stars
Your laughter feels like starlight
And we are not under attack of the world, we are not running from anyone
In this dream, everything is scented with happiness
when you hand me your heart in between my palms and
Before i pinch myself back to reality
I remember how insignificant feeling small is when i'm by your side
I tell you i love you under my breath

I love you. I can't stop saying it. I love you. I love you. & I love you so much.
In this dream, we can confess we love each other,
Nobody ever gets hurt because of love. I want to tell you i missed you,
And I love you more in this dream.
In this dream, we never have to wake up.

3. YOU'RE ALL MY PRAYERS ANSWERED

On days all my tears evaporated to steam, the cuts on my forearm burnt like ripped skin. I found you between the cracks of my soul, without asking for it. Like basking in the arcane light of the moon, you stood there shining like shooting stars.I found you in between the lines of all my favourite songs.How can I ever tell you how much i have fallen in love with you? By which I mean how much i am ready to call you my god, my religion, my reason of survival.In my dream, everytime you walk in through that door in my beating heart, in the middle of my chest where you are the safe space, where your name is endlessYour smile is like liquid starlight brightening my worst days and painting starry nights like the blue in your eyes.i don't know how to write about love without being afraid of ruining it but If this was a love poem, you'd be my muse.

You'd be the amalgamation of all my prayers answered. You're warm pink sunset skies adorned with strands of delicate velvet clouds.

You're a field of flowers disguised as a storm, such that when you look at me, it rains flowers. I'm so scared to touch you, even from miles away because your beauty births art, love embraces you every moment because you're too precious to let go of. But i want to hold your face, in between the space of my palms and kiss the sadness away. Against my cold hands, your heart would shiver, which i would never let go of until the sorrow in your eyes die out and what remains would only be a memory of happiness. A memory of a time when we were together, deeply lost in each other's eyes.

4. I CANNOT FIX YOU BUT I CAN LOVE YOU

The sharp summer heat bores holes j your skin and you look at me expe answers (flowers to your barren landmines). I'm afraid to disappoint you just as much as I'm afraid to hold your heart in my infected palms and scream before I can drop it, "handle with care" i I say before your lips may mumble. I'm afraid to be your mother who was never home and your father who came home late. I'm afraid my two arms are too less of an embrace on cold sweat night. That there might just be too much grief when both of us add up and I will drown in its high tides. I'm afraid that I would be cave more than a home, a hollow belonging and an oxymoron. I'm afraid.

I cannot fix you but But i promise you that I will stick out to fight your cupboard closed demons and bottled-up ghosts of your past i promise you I would sing lullabies to the grief in you and put it to sleep forever if i could. I promise you to play hide and seek with the anxious kid and kiss the wounds away of the teen.I cannot turn diamond under pressure and sew thick skin into your bones so the next time you're alone, you have nothing to be afraid of. I cannot swim oceans for you or bring home stars, but I will love you. I cannot be god, my love, but i will love you like love was the only reason i came to know you.

5. YOUR OCEAN

The moist wind tastes sweet on my cheeks as I look beside me, at you-my ocean. You've always teased the mystery inside me by willing to know more about me but the mystery inside you remains untouched by me as I drown in your teal eyes one more time. It was as if the sky and the sea competed wit each other to paint the best shades of blue and yet effortlessly,you stood there upholding your tides with ease. As the waves go higher and higher, the tides come closer and closer-you hold my hand a bit tighter- as if to fight away all the uncertainties that ever existed. The sand falling out and away from beneath our toes remind me of the passage of the time ive known you-how ive grown up with you-how you've mastered every corner of your creation. And as i keep my head on your shoulder, i remember all of those times when you've had to tread the tempests alone, the times when even I failed to be there with you and it scares me of the future. But I still choose to drown your shadows in your deepest corners of your heart and love you whole like the ocean does to us. I'll be the ocean to you just like youve been to me. I'll drown away your darkest horrifying hours in my saltwater and let you pour your heart out and cry when need be, in my oceans I'll accept you, embrace you and bring to the surface only your favourite memories.

6. LOVE SCENERY

We are walking hand in hand as the sun sets over the lake, and you whisper to me "why do you love me?"

And as words betrays me, i think about the lavender love we have shared over a span of a decade,the blushing from one corner of the classroom to the other corner, even if our eyes met barely. The freaking out moments whenever our hands brushed on each other, leaving butterflies in its wake. The sharing of headphones on our ride back home, songs that have now become the legendary milestones of our love. Reading poetry together as if all the words rolling on your tongue are phrases of love in its purest form. The way you hold my hand, as if to say "I'm here, my love, you have nothing to worry about." The way our fingers interlace as if to say "this will too pass away, you will be whole again" the way your arms open and accept me in my shattered form, never asking for me to become anything more than i already am, as if to say " i will love you so much and so deeply that you will want to love yourself too". The way you hug me tightly drowning me in your silent love, slowly patting my back and whispering "there is nothing to fear, you have been through worse and you'll survive again and again". You untangle my hair strand by strand and put a sunflower by my ear, and the softness of your heart turns into wet flower petals that leave paperhearts on my lips. If there is anything as sweet red as your love, it is you. The way you say nothing yet your words make way into my chaotic heart. The way your eyes light up the flickering lamps of my life. I'm an old grain film and you're my handhold vintage camera that gives meaning to the frail moments of my life. You're my safe place as in the moonlight that falls on the face of my daisies on shadowy nights. You love me like You're the clouds kissing the bluest skies on a clear day, and I'm the void of space adorned in your starlight love.

Why do I love you? There is no reason only the fact that I do. That the way you love me is the only way love has looked beautiful to me. That the way you love makes me want to save myself and stay alive to love you one more day. That forever only seems real when i am with you. That you've taught me how to love the most unlovable of things. We are feathers of the lovebirds who tasted freedom. Because you are the only lullaby i was born to sing, the yellow colour of my blackbody heart.

7. PERHAPS I DONT KNOW HOW TO LOVE

But i will put my ear against your chest to listen to the giggle of your heartbeat and celebrate every lub and dub, every crest and trough of the organ of your living

As i remain in pure awe of how you came to be created, the being worth of so much love that only i would not suffice. I will hold your every ache that your heart has gone through, in between the crumbling lines of my palm like holding a delicate rose still covered with its thundering thorns, i know you're scared.

But i will hold you never to let go, because if i love your bloom i shall love your scars the same.

Perhaps i don't know how to love but I will draw beams of light from the strands of your hair, to make you believe that the sun resides in your being, in your smile that places itself in the corner of your eyes, in your pink gums that reveal itself when you laugh fully from ear to ear, in your scarlet stretch marks that exist in different parts of your body shaped like a crescent moon, reminding you that you too are like the moon, going through phases to be beautiful.

And perhaps i don't know how to love but i will love you like your name is the only synonym of love I've ever known. Honey drips from your eyelashes when you shed tears from the same eyes that see beauty in everything. I will love every part of you like i love the craters of the moon.

Perhaps i don't know how to love but i will hold your hand to my heart and let you listen the reason of my existence is you. Like i will let you hold my pulsating hand when your nightmares haunt you and don't let you sleep, i will let you hug me tight when you can't stop sobbing even if i can't breathe. I will keep calling you day in and day out because i am worried about you. I will text you a billion times to make sure you're eating on time and taking care of yourself. Don't you understand, I'm always worried about you. Because even if i don't know how to love, i still love you. Because i want you to remember me as a sweet aftertaste in your mouth. So that one day when i am no more, you can talk of me with a smile. So that one day, you will know that even though perhaps i never knew how to love , despite it all,it was all worth it.

PART 2

AFTERMATH

-That ache in my chest,

the sound of my heart breaking

8. SUMMER FLOWER

You come to me
Then cry for a long time
"Take care. Let's stop now"
Longing for us from yesterday
When i came back you were gone
Tell me it's not true,
Tell me
We can become
flowers that never wither
Your eyes that used to look at
me
When i try to erase it,
it gets deeper
When you left me,
I knew this summer was over
Tell me you'll come back
I've been hoping
It's not true
Tell me you'll come back to me
We who were dazzling,
Like flowers that never wither
Tell me, tell me
"I'm waiting for you"

9. I'M SORRY, I LOVED YOU

Why did you have to leave me like that
The door open behind you, blood dripping from my fingertips
Scars burning on your forearms, all the wounds i blew gold into while i held the fire far too long
What went wrong, Why did we end like this,
I need to reply, you expect an answer, i need to and my reflexes say "It's astronomy"
"We're two worlds apart"
Two storms enraged as two hearts were deranged
This. Was the aftermath of a summer love
I envy how the roses are brave, they bear the thorns even in the graves.
Hearing you cry on the phone, i remember to breathe in your sobs, so that i never forget the consequences of us
while a part of me died last night, but i will not mourn- because it's not about me
This poem is you- you are the poem i didn't ever get the guts to write
See how we're trying to not hurt while we tear each other apart, who knew while i sewed your holes back together - i would increase my own
But trust me darling, it's not your fault, when i sunk in your eyes and forgot breathing keeps one alive
Right person, wrong time- wrong person, right time, we were a tragedy to begin with- let this be our eulogy. This is me holding a candle to my face, setting fire to the mess i made- letting you go is the best i can do

But i don't want to. This can't be the end. Voice quivering, knees breaking, veins pulsating, heart throbbing- let's not end.
There is a potential to goodbyes, to break or make a being into a human
But what name do we give to this much grief?
I'm so scared, of so many things that i can no longer love- the only mistake we didnt make, was run. As i kept trying to heal you- to bring the shine back in your nights- so that i didn't repeat your family line, i mustve stayed too long, I've begun to look like you
But ive been holding my breath under water for an year
Just looking at the sunrise in your eyes
Just hoping it gets better eventually
But now i can hear my planets cry
They are telling me to stop lying
Do you call this a home?
When our lungs decay though there's so much air?
And so i slash my flesh at every place i can, wishing it didn't have to be this tough
I can't believe I'm telling you this, I'm sorry this is not a good apology
When all I can give you anymore is dead flowers- a book of regrets- and tears that seas won't be enough to suffice for.
I will remember you in every poem that writes itself, every beat of all my favourite songs, every smile on a happy day yet
Some things aren't meant forever-i only hope you forget me, hate me, spite me, never forgive me. After all, what killed us couldn't have made us stronger- i couldn't be the goddess you chose to worship instead if our love was a war, i became your most painful wound.
But i hope when you remember us- you remember me happy, giggling
Darling, it's not your fault so let's stop trying to keep us alive,

You're pointing at the stars in the sky that have already died.
Maybe you saved me- maybe the sky looked nice today- maybe this is the only perfect goodbye- because love isn't enough
I'm sorry, but i loved you.

10. THINGS I WISH I COULD TELL YOU BUT I DONT

1. I'm staring holes into the couple sitting across me on the bus/ they look cute/ holding hands/ fingers intertwined like how we used to be the gaps between a my fingers are ghosts that singing of loneliness.

2. My eyes are always searching for you, in empty apartment rooms, in the right side of my bed, in the cold drops of November rains, in the increasing holes under my ribcage,in broken cups, In stranger's backs, in the shove of a shoulder in metro, in eyes of new people, in the aftertaste of October skies in my mouth, in the night skies devoid of stars, in craters of Earth's only moon, in the scratch of old cardigans, in the pages of my torn diaries, in shedding of my skin.

3. I'd crawl and scrape my knees to be near you but the only thing left of you is crumpled newspapers and fresh bruises on my knees/ they don't hurt just like our love died a coldblooded death/ just like you always left the door open when you used to leave/ just like you were always leaving/ just like I'm still tugging at you sweatshirt from behind asking you to not go/ you tiptoe out of my bedroom so that you don't wake people up/ but I'm awake, night after night, trying to remember how your voice sounded in my ears/ how your leaving made no difference to the scent of you in my hands

4.Fall is the time our spring bloomed, but it was before every October that our love
smelled of dying/We were kids with pink noses and burnt fingers from sniffing the
cold in the air while we leaped into fires/fires, we were never afraid of/ we loved
burns too much that our love was aflame and we didn't even notice like a burnt child
running barefoot into a forest fire/ Where are you now when I've become a flicker.

5. I no longer ask of you to be my soulmate/ couldn't we have just still been something that is not dead(read: Acquaintances) How do you spell "i love you" when you really want to say "I have walked over molten lava and it hurt more when you say goodbye"/how to become whole when a part of you leaves everytime the sun sets in the northern sky/ how to make amends when our love was had holes in the heart to begin with?/ How to love me when I'm a girl with a bullet wound in her chest?/our spot by the river is now a crime scene. This, the last time i will think of you and i in the same sentence/ because i look at you, and all i see is red. Red like the marks of your hand left in mine, red like the flowers that withered by our last anniversary, red like the flame this love burns on, red like the lines on my flesh every night while your name echoes in my heart beat, red like the toxicity we have become for each other, red like you and i you and i you and-..

11. THINGS TO SAY INSTEAD OF "LETS BREAK UP"

Our love is now, complete.

Even if we are left with open wounds and burning bruises- it is time to let go of my hand.

My support isn't reaching you anymore, love.

Your heart is no longer my warm embrace.

These arms are not holding me but they have become my restrictions.

I loved you with my whole heart even when you couldn't and that is okay this is me loving you enough to let you walk away.

There are so many things i want to say but it has all lost meaning now.

i will think about you but I won't be telling you anymore.

I will always have a part of me left in you and a part of you left in me.

I will always love you regardless of who I'm with or where i am/ i will always love you.

"There will come a day when flowers will stop blooming from the touch of your name on my lips. There will come a day when i will no longer contemplate our love. There will come a day when the sun will sleep with your name beneath and their will be silence when instead of our names spoken side-by-side

12. COPING WITHOUT YOU HERE.

Now you're the title of every heartbreak poem i write. Your name tattooed on the back of my palms. Your smell surrounds my heart in a wounded embrace. I still hum your favourite song like an anthem to my loneliness. If love was all you ever asked for, then why couldn't i be enough? I ask myself the same question again and again on your birthday each year. On my saddest days, the air mimicks your laughter and in two seconds, I'm but a puddle of water and i pretend to not drown once again. but in reality, love is a lie- and I'm but your greatest hypocrite. Two summers back, i told you I loved you and come November, our love turned blue from the cold in our hearts. Couldn't you pick enough flowers from my chest when you finally went away? Now they are rotting inside the hole left in your wake. We were two coward lovers in this delusion kind of love story, bestfriends to lovers was the worst possible trope. I envy being a child again, so i wouldn't have to give a name to this feeling. How do you survive sinking if you're carrying the heaviest burden on your chest? Even if i cut myself, this gravity won't let me go. Now I'm no longer a person but cracks through which your memory seeps in- a body haunted by your touch. We were two lovers in the dark staring at the sunrise in each other's eyes and praying for it to light the way. Maybe it was when i no longer tended to your sadness instead of mine. Maybe it was when we showed each other the naked problems breeding under our skin. Maybe it was when love became the problem bleeding from our internal organs. Maybe the celestial bodies made this happen or maybe it all started when we held hands the very first time or the time you held me tight from collapsing or maybe we planned it all from the beginning, and now all that's left of us is a fleeting history.

13. YOUR NAME IS A FLAME IN MY THROAT

1) I still find myself wishing you would show up at my door, with roses faded of colour and cheeks stained with tear- lines. I promise I will no longer complain about how chaotic you look or how sweaty your hands are, I don't care anymore-I just want to be held one more time in your embrace-even if its wounded or empty, just like me.

2) I loved a boy and now I cant make art without ruining myself first. The spaces in between my fingers reek of longing,and every time I try to write about love- I come home to you,but I miss you more than I remember you by which I mean I am sorry for every time I yearn for you.

3) Your name is a flame in my throat and it tastes like goodbye. Every night I dream of another world where you and I could be spelled in the same sentence even if not side by side. I loved you in another life because I cannot love you in this one. I still get lost in the tenderness with which you used to pronounce my name, with lilies blooming on the tip of your tongue,

4) The stars talk about us in hushed tones, while the universe is quite ever since you walked away. Maybe this is how our story never ends, maybe this is our forever-cold and unkind, from the look in your eyes-you did not even turn back for the one last time so i stared holes into

your broad back until my eyes ached, until the only thing i could do was cry.

14. TEN THINGS THAT MAKE ME MISS YOU MORE EACH DAY

1. My ripped palms, open like a gaping wound long for the embrace of yours like sunflowers yearning for the April summer sun. The tanned lines of fate resting on my hands wrote you a love letter but you will never know.

2. Your old space themed tshirt rotting in the corner of the second drawer of my cupboard, stained of the popsicles that were your favourite in June smells like the dream where you never stopped chasing behind me.

3.. The French perfume that i never got tired of, something that reminds me of the consequences of loving recklessly-getting lost under the starlight when our heartbeats rushed and faces blushed, we promised that we would not let go of each other until the end of the earth.

4. My freckles-and how you kissed them to beauty like dipping our toes in the lakes of the craters of the moon. How you loved to caress every scar like peeling an orange, layer by layer- deep but tender

5. Couple rings that we bought for each other, now cries for the both of us guilty of not being able to make you stay.

6. The earrings you gifted me when we were still in middle school,how it resembled the rings of Saturn and now it's just a reminder of the distance between Saturn and its moon, like me and you.

7.Falling leaves remind me of your eyelashes and the way stars would land on them everytime you shed a single tear. I still get lost in the galaxies bound in your eyeballs though they will never again look for me.

8. Every gift you gave me on each of my birthdays, like a reminder of how our existence intertwined with each other until one day when there no longer seemed enough reasons to hold on.

9. The keyring you brought from your vacation with my name engraved on it still spells my name out in capital letters like the last text you ever sent me.

10. My heart, the organ that misses you the most is cold from not being touched by which I mean it starved itself ever since it could no longer be an instrument for your love.

15. IM AT WAR WITH MYSELF, FOR YOU

Our love was a mistake to begin with. Every step i took towards you was responded with waves that pushed you miles away from us, like the distance between star clusters that will never spell forever. Your love is not mine for the taking so I'm becoming a thief in the night. I no longer know how to spell your name without spelling grief first. I loved a boy and that's it. That was the ruin of every wish we placed on falling stars. And i find myself wondering how much did I really even mean to you? Did I even mean anything? Because your silence seeps into my soul and crushes my bones. I always saw you in past tense because that's when you fell in love with me. And when i thought i knew your heart well, you made sure i didn't. You made sure to call me close but keep me away at an arm's length, the distance between my love and your eyes. And now I'm at war with myself.for you. Do you remember? When we stayed up nights pretending we were laying still, side by side underneath a sky full of stars - with spring blooming around us. Only if you had told me back then, the stars in the heavens have already died.

Just like me and you and our embrace.

16. MUSCLE MEMORY

There are days i wake up with my heart racing, there's a huge hole in my chest where you used to be. There is something in my soul that remembers you more than it misses you And these days i call it muscle memory.I wonder why my hands smell of blood when they have been used to smelling of your perfume. Little did I know love is the sharp pain that won't stop, that's the constant ache in your chest that won't go away easily. Washing my hands furiously only causes my skin to open up, it's like when you finally stop an itch and you realize it's because you've ripped a hole in your skin. Then there are days i try to take all the words you left me with and fit them like pieces of a puzzle into the hole in my chest. But there will only be an excess of poems that i can write of you, you are the excuse to my poetry. I wonder why my legs always take me to the porch infront of the house that is yours. When can I finally stop thinking about you? All my thoughts have the same address, that is yours. Do the stars twinkle, where you are, the same way as it does for me? They won't stop shining like the shooting stars that fell from your eyes when you were leaving. There are days when my skin hugs me back pretentiously and it is nothing like the embrace of your arms on long lonely nights. How easily I'd collapse in between your arm's length. How easily I'd melt into your shadows. Even my shadows sob into the night these days. They are tired of following me around with their partner lost. They no longer feel the need to exist just like me, myself and i. The gaps between my fingers have exhausted their breath singing of their loneliness, haunted by your presence. Your fading hands touch mine in a familiar way to escape this labyrinth of suffering, only to realise again and again that it's not you. But just a whiff of you is enough to bring back memories i thought i had forgotten. I didn't just love you with my brain, I loved you with my mind and my body. And none of them wants to forget you even if I am ready to. But How do I say i miss you when i was the one who ended it? I wonder if it is even love if i didn't fall?

17. ON THE RADIO

On the radio, it sounds like a tempest is brewing. The end of the world is coming nearer
On the radio, they don't know about us yet.
They don't know the number of cuts on my wrist from loving you
They don't know the oceans of blue in my room from holding on to you They don't know i fell deeper when i stopped loving you more than i should
On the radio, the world hasn't ended yet.
On the radio, we are still together like a forever The skies are a burning pink and have not stopped blushing since you last showed up in a suit. It has been raining in my city non stop ever since I last held you in my arms, because both of us knew it was wounded, a wounded embrace. The grass cannot be greener on the other side because the other side doesn't exist. Everything here smells of dying, anyway. Everything smells of your last touch. Everything sings the words you left me with in our last kiss.
"You will regret this"
"You will regret not loving me"
"You will regret ending it first"
I wake up wondering why everything is the same as it was, why life keeps going on the way it does despite my wish to kill myself every moment. Why do I keep crying when i hear your name? Why can't I stop whispering your name during my utter breakdown? I was wrong. My
world has ended long back, My world ended when i lost your love.

18. IT IS RAINING IN MY CITY

It is raining in my city and i can't help but think of you And i imagine somewhere someone has a broken heart. Somewhere someone's tears are getting shed unnoticed. But I'm here thinking of your fingertips. left cold eversince the last time i held them. There is no one to fill the gap between adjacent fingers, i can only hope the weather isn't too harsh on your bleeding heart. I'm thinking of your white laced umbrella that you'd usually forget to take with yourself while going out on days like this. On days like this, you'd usually forget everything that loves you and gives you a reason to live on. On days like this, it is cold and there is no one to warm your hands like i did. Tell me, on days like this i do you remember me? But I'm here thinking of your sneakers that i gifted you on your fifteenth birthday, only today they would probably get soaked and soggy from the rainwater collecting in the gaps, like in between your cheekbone and eyebrow. But i hope its not unbearable. I hope you find a way out through this rainy day, holding on to fleeting moments as memories of the love you felt. I hope the thunder is not too loud to drown out your own voice. But I'm here thinking of the times you'd sing lullabies to me and put me to sleep while i stayed afraid of the world. I hope that there is someone to lull you to sleep today, someone who knows how much you're afraid of the thundering clouds. Someone who accepts your heart's cries like the earth accepts the rain. And I'm still thinking of the way you'd hold the rain in between the space of your palms and carry it delicately just like the way you held my tears in that safe space. Tell me, does someone hold you that way? Do you feel safe like you used to back then? Does it sometimes make you want to run away too? Does it really not haunt you, whatever we had?

Because it's raining in my city and I can't help but think of you. Maybe somewhere someone is crying their heart out. Somewhere someone just wants to cry out for once. And all I can say for now is you're my rainwater and I'm clearly drowning.

19. ON TURNING PRETTY BOYS INTO POETRY

(1) Pretty boy grows flowers instead of hands. He touches my freckles by which i mean wounds, with palms that are softer than rose petals and with it leaves me smelling like blossoms in spring. Spring blushes infront of pretty boy like she is grateful to be owned by him one more year. Holding hands with pretty boy is no longer enough for my barbed wire soul, i need to hold his heart in between the gaps of my palms and kiss every ache and fill every crack with gold-weave kintsugi.

(2) Pretty boy has a broken soul,reeking of childhood trauma and memories of abuse,but i can fix him. i just dont try hard enough- i just havent held him like a moon in its waxing phase yet, i just havent embraced his scars like their mine own-like they belong to the home in my soul-i just havent written a loveletter to the fire yet. Maybe im scared i will only find the boy lighting flames to every home he has been to.

(3) Pretty boy is delusional. He weaves stories out of thin air like he lives within the clouds and rides on the wind. No matter how many times i tell him, he refuses to believe that this world is dystopian and that the wind can be brutal- the breeze bruises my feelings and then he kisses them goodnight and tells me to stop imagining things.

(4) Pretty boy has trust issues but he falls in love with everything, including non existent creatures like me. And he loves me like i'm his moon and sun but he leaves me when I least expect it, then calls it astronomy. Then blames it on the stars for being dead for so long because now his wishes cant be resurrected. He leaves the door open when he walks away from me, and my gaping open arms. He tells me to fall in love with the emptiness instead of him- but only if i could go back in time just to see his face one last time.

(5) Pretty boy is the title of every poem i write, every verse that echoes in my mind like a silent reminder that pretty boys are an embodiment of unconditional love that is inevitable to meet an end. I beg him to forgive me, to spit me out and curse me a hundred times because my love wasnt enough for someone like him, pretty boy smiles. And whispers behind my ears, "write me something pretty".

20. THE LAST POEM

This is the last time i will hold you
In between the spaces of my palm like holding the sun and letting my palms burn from the heat
like the heat of your burning heart in my pyre of love
This is the last time you will exist as my lover,like the love slipping away from in between the spaces of my fingers like blossoms blooming on my lips from your name have translated into our last kiss.
This is the last time we will be whole
Together and half,apart because this is the last time we will fit like puzzles that were never meant to be together in the first place
Th is the last time you will be engraved in my words like sipping honey from the brown of your eyes that would melt me into water
Like basking in your starlight, whenever you'd close your eyes and pretend to sleep only so that i could stare at you a little more
Like dripping in the rain whenever you would leave my hand, in the middle of a conversation
Like taking turns at guessing what the other half is thinking because we knew how to read minds by this time, because i was your first love and your last mistake made in the illusion of painting a happy memory
This will be the last time i will immortalize you in my verses, i swear
This will have to be the last time
The last time i am yours

21. AN AUTOPSY OF LOVE

For a few days after the point in my life where I realised that
You were busy starring in someone else's life
Someone, who became your savior in the aftermath of me
I wondered have you or have you not thought of me even once? And soon
I couldn't breathe. I was on life support.
I kept wondering if my role was of the only one in your life
Or just the other one?
I wasn't sure if the blood I spit every now and then was just vomit or an indicator of something worse
Eventually they called me to that room,
the one where no one else wanted to go to
The room where the doctor looked like grim reaper
His judgment was that "the love is gone"
And I knew, all that's left was just cancer.
Remnants of a love that was born with a hole in its heart
Some nights I was ready to give in to death's whispers
They were far too tempting,
Even better than when you held my hand
Because I don't even remember how I felt then. It was too long ago.
I feel stupid for calling it love all this time
Because how can this be love?
How can it ask for my life ? With what audacity?

And why should I give everything I ever held close to my soul for something as fickle and untrue as this?
Because if you meant it when you said you loved me, you wouldn't have moved on this quick.
You wouldn't have been okay with me hurting this much, when every single moment I breathed - I choked- I know
You didn't love me. You didn't love me. You didn't love me. You rip my heart to cradle it in your arms oh- You don't know how precious love is, how beautiful it is supposed to make you feel, it is not supposed to make you want to cut yourself to let love go for once and for all
Atleast now I can answer myself in the mirror. All this while, I've been waiting
I've been waiting for kindness since I was born
I was hurting, unnoticed, silently all this time.
Begging for forgiveness when I did nothing wrong.
When the reflection asks me "did you love him more or did he?"
I can now smile and say I did.
That's why it hurts this much.
That's why I stopped talking to you that night, hands trembling but I left yours first.
Knees wobbly, head dizzy.
I couldnt think straight all I knew was I have come too far to give up now
I see the way I bleed
Had stars rearranging in the skies above
The doctor put me off the life support yesterday. High on this pain that is life, I'm moving on. I'm not sorry for how I look at us. It was unkind. It was cold.

I am used to being alone during the rains these days, maybe the cancer is not in my heart but my brain
I want to breathe. Desperately. Genuinely.
The doctor asks me my symptoms.
In an effort to open my mouth to break the silence that engulfed me the only thing I say is even if love was there, it did not survive.
All that remained were tear stained cheeks and bruises that can never be seen.
The death certificate was issued in the name of love, while I lived on in the realm of mortals.

22. ARE WE IN A DREAM?

I wish all of this was a dream
I wish loving you didn't ask things from me that i can never give
I wish loving you was easier than the hate i endorse for myself
But most days i wish i had loved me first, before i loved you.
I will try to not starve myself,
Just because i think you're mad at me
I will try to not drown myself,
Because it's better than seeing you leave.
I wish loving you didn't take parts of me
And leave bruises in its wake
I wish loving you didnt poke holes in my ribcage
I will try to not fall sick so often
So that you don't have an excuse to think of me
Did you eat today?

Cause i didn't
I still think you're mad at me.
All my friends are missing me but I'm busy looking at you still "typing" on the other side of the screen
But its okay, it's fine, this is love, I'm in love.
Maybe this is what happens when you fall in love
I've left them all behind. I'm busy falling in love with you.
Maybe I've starved myself a little,maybe I'm still
Maybe I'm the problem, all it takes for you to fall in love with me

But you'll never know, and you'll never love me.

Part 3

LET LOVE HEAL

Coming home to yourself, picking yourself up and allowing yourself to give love another chance.

23. YOU WERE RIGHT

You were right,
you are too much for my heart.
I no longer know if I love you or not, I completely lost it it seems.
Ever since you left, I discovered and rediscovered myself.
I worked all day and kept myself busy just because I don't want to think about you. Or about what happened to us. To me.
I even stopped writing about love altogether because
Writing about love meant writing about a tragedy. About the grief sitting in the middle of my chest.
You see I'm trying
I'm trying my best
To heal.
To be okay again.

I'm trying my best to forget you
Forget the storm you were in my peace
The rain in my summer
The cold breeze in winter
The hand that warmed up mine
The lyrics to my favorite song
Nowadays I am afraid to ask what is love anymore, I'm scared it will lead me back to you
But I swear I'm trying
I'm trying to tell myself that
it is okay to be in love and still grow apart

It is okay to be in love with someone and not be able to accept the love back
It is okay to not be able reciprocate sometimes
To start to hate loving anything. To not know what love is.
It is okay
It will be okay
Someday the hole in my heart will completely stitch itself back
The cuts won't sting like it did in the past
The anger won't be as hot as it was
The tears will dry out before the rainy days hit again and
There will be spring in town
I will not look back when we walk away from each other
This is me right where you left me
I'll pick up the pieces shattered on the floor
I'll shut my eyes and let you go
And all I'll be left with is a smile,
Pasted across my face
Saying "even now,
I'm so glad I met you"

//People can change. Feelings can change.
But that doesn't mean the love that once brought them together never existed
It only means that when people grow, they sometimes grow apart//

24. VALENTINE'S DAY

This valentine's day, I'm unclenching my fists. Loosening my posture. Relaxing my shoulders.

The sun is setting in the horizon

This valentine's day, I am pausing.

There is no rush. The lights still flicker in the distant cafes. It shows red on the signal, everyone has paused and it's just us two humans crossing each other by

Imagine this letter to be a glitch in space-time because

I know this valentine no one will drop by with a bouquet of sunflowers because only you'd know it's my favourite

but that's okay

I know this time around no one will give me a surprise video call at 12 AM only to goof around in the middle of the night

I know nobody will sing me lullabies so I can sleep in peace on their lap

I know I won't have a shoulder to cry on, a hand to hold, an embrace to find my refuge in, a hug to crumble into

I won't have a valentine this year,

or the next maybe

Even if I did, it won't be you.

It won't be your long tender pianist-ish fingers interlaced in mine,or your laughter in that hoarse voice ringing in my ears or you forgetting to bring something for the nth time or the afterglow of your pale red colored shirt, pleated matched with black pants and black formal shoes looking like a lover's long lost kiss, it won't be your Radiohead

and The Smiths, and I won't be around when you scream "MAMA OOO"(bohemian Rhapsody Ref.) in your blue room with glass shot full of tears instead of beer
This valentine I shall forgive everything that went wrong
Everything that was a mishap a disaster
I will learn to heal again
This valentine I'm remembering your presence by honouring your absence
I will leave rose petals in the wake when
I wash the blood off my hands for real.
I will shed off your fragrance that had enveloped me all these years
This valentine I'm letting you go
Because I've always just wanted
you to be happy
And for the last time
that is what makes me the
happiest.

25. LOVE, ONCE AGAIN

To the next boy who walks into my life with a palm full of love-

I know I haven't met you yet.
I don't yet know how your name tastes in my mouth
I don't yet know how the moonlight sculpts your face against the night sky
And I don't even know how your voice melts in my ears
But here's what I do know-
what I can warn you about me
You see I am convinced after all this time
That I am indeed very difficult to love. Tell me why
People would always leave me first
Even when I give them all of me every single time
Heart by heart?
Or maybe, let's just assume
That love itself is just bad for my mental health.
For as silly as it sounds
Uptil now, it's been the only emotion wrecking me up
Like a thunderstorm on good hair days
But even when I say this, I hope you don't believe me
I hope you don't believe when I say I will never fall in love again.
I know, I know I spell love the wrong way
Sometimes I have nothing to show for it but
Will you trust me if I said being a nonbeliever,
I still pray for you when I see the rainbow after first rains

Will you trust me when I plant landmines around my fragile heart
because I'd rather walk on broken glass around you
instead of knowing that you don't feel the same way about me
And if we never become anything, what will you remember me by?
Well, I like to believe that there are bigger infinites
Where we could be just about anything
And I'm sure by the time you're reading this
You'd have already turned into poetry
Because poetry is afterall, for fools like me
Who spend their entire lives scared of being loved
And dipping their toes in the ocean of love
I'm sorry that this poem keeps stretching out into the universe
I'm afraid that even anatomy can't explain this feeling anymore
I'm convinced, that I will always crave for love to heal me
Even when I don't believe in it.
And when I say I'll never love anyone again
With tears dead in my eyelids
Sure, I may be a hypocrite.
But tell me just why must you be this
Loveable?

26. DO I EVEN DESERVE LOVE?

I wake up another day
Drenched in my own sweat,
choking on stale tears and breathing
on borrowed time
I drag my body out of my bed and drag it across the living room into the kitchen
My feet falters, my body trembles,
I realise how depression holds me hostage one more day
At this point im ready to beg her to press the trigger
At this point I can't believe in a hope with her wings cutoff and a tumour engulfing her heart
I spill blood every time I take my lover's name
Love will not heal me.
It can't clot the open wounds on my skin
It can't stitch back happiness to my memory
It can't stop me from crumbling every time someone is kind to me
Love will not heal me
For when I hold my lover's hand, I'm afraid depression is trying a noose around my neck
For when I try to run away, I only trip over my own broken selves
All the hurt I hide away under the moonlight
Breathes behind my smile,
Begging to be seen for once without judgement
But when that day comes

I am afraid
I won't be able to stand straight, won't be able to say how much I love you in the same breath that will be my last
I will still be afraid of the possibility
That someday I too might deserve something as precious as love
And kindness
And happiness
And everything that is beautiful
Even when it's vulnerable.
This poem is not a love letter
It's a suicide note
Every love poem I've ever written is so
My lover's looking at me
And I don't have the courage to hold his face in my palms and tell him
I'll be here forever, beside him
Sharing the same air
I am a woman with rope marked neck
And bleeding wrists
A woman with scars on her chest from trying to rip her heart out every time
It beats too loud in her eardrums
I'm a woman with a past buried six feet under
deeper than the conspiracy theories of the world
You should not love me
I am unlovable, I am raw, I am ugly
Pains of my life painted in red on my face
While I smear black to hide away from
All the light
I'm the shadows without a name

Hiding is my only comfort, and my safe space
You should leave before I become your ruin
Another love that couldn't live through the light of the day
Another love that could not save me
That is the only fate carved underneath my skin
The only life in which I'm happy
Does not have the will to survive
As much I can endure.

27. IF THE WORLD WAS ENDING TONIGHT

Dearest,

The sun is setting in the horizon
The sky is painted a vermillion red
The colour of your face that used to blush
On hearing my name
The birds are flying away from the face of the earth
Far away to somewhere where peace exists
Love exists
Without the need of a beginning or an ending
My heart beats slowly, it no longer rushes behind your touch
Everything is calm; right before the storm.
I no longer know if the storm has washed over me
Or if there is more to come
I know this
That the world is ending
My lover is no longer beside me.
If this love was a mistake to begin with
Then what about all the kindness we gave to this world
All the time we spent in each other's embrace
All the child like giggling of our hearts?
The flowers that bloomed when we grew closer
That brought spring before winter ended
What if all of this is a mistake
Then you and I should no longer mean anything

I can not live on by the strands of an almost
And uncertainty that is always ending
And a beginning that never started
I'm afraid
Not because the apocalypse threatens
Not because my home was destroyed
And is now just rubble
But because your hand is no longer intertwined in mine
Your touch is now my scarcity
Your voice is deafening to my ears
But they still beg to hear
And melt in your presence
My lips spell your name
When death comes to take me away
When does a lover die they say?
When their love writes a suicide note
When it has been too much
Just enough
To give it all up
But I still wait by the dissolving skyline
The vermillion red reflected in your eyes
I imagine you beside me
Holding my heart
Before it all ends
Before we say goodbye
Can I hug you one last time
One last kiss to Seal what we had
Hide it forever in time oblivion
No one will ever love you the way I did.

No one will love me the way you do
Let time and space be the judge
If our love is True
This love will save the world from collapsing on us today
This love will heal the pains of tomorrow
This love will keep the world spinning
Spinning around
As we perish.

28. RAIN IS MY FAVOURITE SEASON.

They say you see the size of your love on one of those rainy days it doesn't stop pouring
Was that the reason none of us had the courage to open the umbrella over another's head?
Or was it because our love spanned the skies above
That we decided to get drenched together
Like all the thunderstorms we endured hand in hand?
Like all the lives we lived till now
These days, I feel the weight of love
And I understand it weighs down on your two shoulder
That it's uncomfortable
Even annoying even
To face something that is larger than you
On a daily basis
But what about those secret glances
When you look at me during the silences in between our conversations
What about the goodnights and good mornings
You were the last person I talked to
And the first person I greeted
If it wasn't anything, then why did you hold me so close to your heart?
Why did you allow me to listen to your heartbeat race against mine?
Why did you hush my tears
And
Entered the lanes of my heart without warning?

If this means nothing, then why did you look at me like that?
Like even if the world ended, it didn't matter
Like all it mattered was, us and what we had
Something precious, delicate and fragile that we shared and kindled between our fingertips
If it all was for nothing,
Why did you travel 30 kilometres just to meet me?
Tell me if I'm overthinking?
Tell me if I'm misinterpreting?
Like the verses of rabindrasangeet
You came into my life like
jhoro hawa(harsh winds)
And now
I'm nothing
Nothing but
An instrument that breathes on your love.
And I'm afraid,
I'm just afraid if you leave
Will I forget how the air tasted
before you came into my life?
Will I ever be able to love again?

29. AUGUST

August was the month when I met you,
A strong wind that tasted sweet and
left me in warm tears
That is how I'd remember him I'd say
The one I used to paint portraits of at night
And I stood there under the street lights
Begging in my mind
Screaming turn around,
Turn around
Hold me before September takes over.

You walked into the room full of unknown names
Like an auburn leaf waltzing through ordinary greens
All this while, I called myself fall
But I only knew what it meant when I heard you whisper it in the drizzling rain
When you hugged me back when the tide hit
And the salt in my tears were strong enough to scar your chest
You were afraid. I was afraid.
But we didn't let it stop us.
And so couldn't we have survived the storm?
I keep asking questions that make lips bleed
You keep answering them
To stop the bleeding you cover my mouth but
It's the end of summer and I'm still aching?

Tell me it was not a dream.
Tell me it was more real than anything could be
Because at least it was for me.

August slips away from the gaps between my fingers
And I realize how truly afraid I am of everything that was happening
Of how I had no control over it
And I imagine you to hold me from crumbling
Stop the passage of time and fight back all the space we've created between us
I used to think if there was anything that is going to destroy me
I'd rather let it be you

When I held your face in my palm
For a moment, were you mine?
Just for those seven whole seconds?
But here is me without your embrace
And I say to you, in confidence
with a tear hiding in my eyelids
I say, I'll manage without you and
Everything that made you up
Will now be just a figment of my imagination
If there was ever an us, it must've been fiction
You see we can never both be real and in love in the same space and time and in August and without breaking each other's hearts and also holding each other through the wind that carries us away from each other because

This is not a fortunate accident and

So many things cannot exist in the same sentence
So this poem will have to end
In the process of not trying to turn you into literature
In the attempt of loving you
Or Almost.
//The waves of the ocean dissolve our names together
As if they never existed in the first place
In the same story.
In another universe,
Would it have been different?
Would we have survived, dearest
August? //

30. WHEN LOVE ARRIVES

When love arrives
You'd think love will always be perfect
Always have a peak sense of fashion and style
Or wear the right boots with the right pair of jeans
Or wear her hair open or tied up in a messy bun the way you want it
Or have a way of speaking that would blow your mind
But you are naive
Because love has no obligation to be according to what you want it to be
Because love just is.
And you love them despite and bec of how different they are
So they might not be wearing their best outfit on the first date
Or they might fidget and stutter and move their legs too much
Or they might not want a relationship, but still want to be with you
Or vice versa
They may keep their hair in a bun even though you like it open because it's what makes them feel more comfortable
They may love the colour red
No matter how much you hate it
They may hate the colour blue
No matter how much you love it
Or they may have a favorite colour you can't even pronounce
A favourite dish you've never tasted
They may dream in a language you don't understand

Yes, love is difficult.
Love is tough
And
Choosing to love will always take strength
But Love is different from everything else
And it is worth it
Even when your heart breaks everytime
Even when they cheat with someone else
When they leave without a word
When they never choose you
When they never love you back
Love is still worth it.
You will always learn something when you give your heart away
And even if it breaks. It will heal and bloom into a new version of you
The one that knows that when love arrives
You are only meant to hold it gently on your palms
Not too tight because it will suffocate otherwise
Just enough so that it does not fall and shatter
Just enough to give it some warmth
And say "thank you for being here,
Thank you for stopping by"

www.ingramcontent.com/pod-product-compliance
Lightning Source LLC
LaVergne TN
LVHW021201160826
845679LV00024B/2204